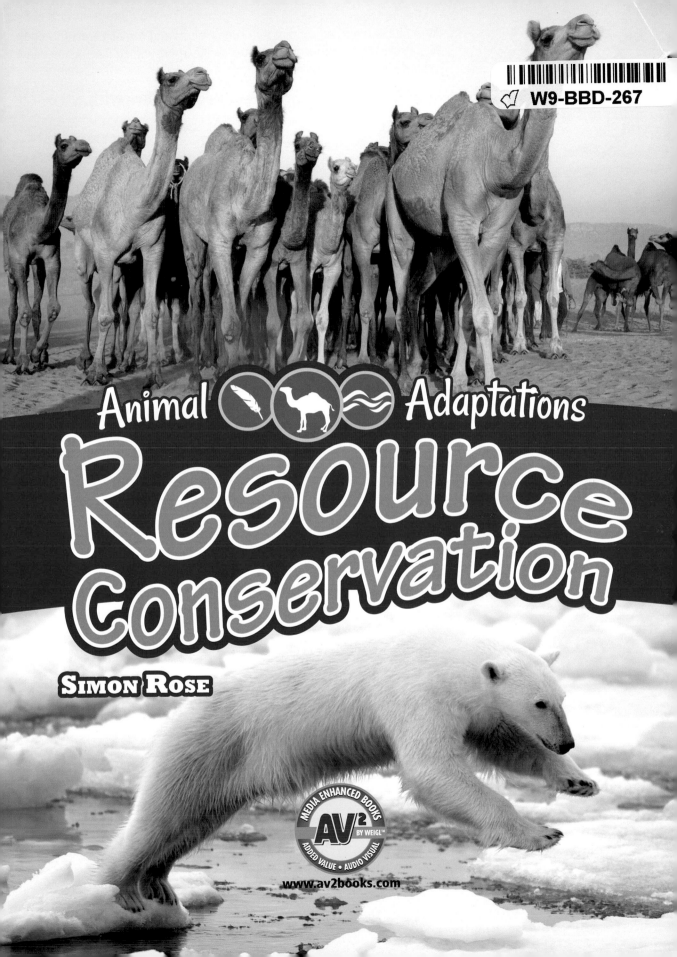

Animal Adaptations

Resource Conservation

Simon Rose

MEDIA ENHANCED BOOKS
AV2 BY WEIGL
ADDED VALUE · AUDIO VISUAL

www.av2books.com

AV² provides enriched content that supplements and complements this book. Weigl's AV² books strive to create inspired learning and engage young minds in a total learning experience.

Your AV² Media Enhanced books come alive with...

Audio
Listen to sections of the book read aloud.

Key Words
Study vocabulary, and complete a matching word activity.

Video
Watch informative video clips.

Quizzes
Test your knowledge.

Embedded Weblinks
Gain additional information for research.

Slide Show
View images and captions, and prepare a presentation.

Try This!
Complete activities and hands-on experiments.

... and much, much more!

Go to **www.av2books.com**, and enter this book's unique code.

BOOK CODE

R 2 4 8 8 9 9

AV² by Weigl brings you media enhanced books that support active learning.

Published by AV² by Weigl
350 5th Avenue, 59th Floor
New York, NY 10118
Website: www.av2books.com

Library of Congress Cataloging-in-Publication Data
Rose, Simon, 1961- author.
 Resource conservation / Simon Rose.
    pages cm. -- (Animal adaptations)
Includes index.
 ISBN 978-1-4896-3683-6 (hard cover : alk. paper) -- ISBN 978-1-4896-3684-3 (soft cover : alk. paper) -- ISBN 978-1-4896-3685-0 (single user ebook) -- ISBN 978-1-4896-3686-7 (multi-user ebook)
 1. Animal behavior--Juvenile literature. 2. Adaptation (Physiology)--Juvenile literature. 3. Adaptation (Biology)--Juvenile literature.
 I. Title. II. Series: Animal adaptations (AV2 by Weigl)
 QL751.5.R67 2016
 591.5--dc23
                            2015000833

Printed in the United States of America in Brainerd, Minnesota
1 2 3 4 5 6 7 8 9   19 18 17 16 15

052015
WEP051515

Project Coordinator Aaron Carr
Art Director Terry Paulhus

Every reasonable effort has been made to trace ownership and to obtain permission to reprint copyright material. The publishers would be pleased to have any errors or omissions brought to their attention so that they may be corrected in subsequent printings.

Photo Credits
Weigl acknowledges Getty Images as its primary photo supplier for this title.
Page 13, bottom left, courtesy of J.M. Storey, Carleton University.

Contents

AV² Book Code 2

What Is an Adaptation? 4

What Is Resource Conservation? ... 6

How Do Animals Use
Resource Conservation? 8

Types of
Resource Conservation 10

How Does It Work? 12

Timeline 14

How Humans Use
Resource Conservation 16

Resource Conservation
and Biodiversity 18

Conservation 20

Activity 21

Quiz 22

Key Words/Index 23

Log on to www.av2books.com 24

What Is an Adaptation?

Many animals have features that help them to survive in their natural **habitat**. These features are known as adaptations. There are a number of reasons for adaptations, such as survival in extreme heat and cold, finding food, avoiding predators, and finding a mate. Adaptations happen over thousands or even millions of years. If an adaptation is successful, parents pass the **genes** for it on to their offspring. The adaptation will help the **species** survive. This process is called **natural selection**.

Some animals live in areas where food and water are scarce for long periods. It is very important for such animals to conserve resources such as fat and water in the body. Any type of adaptation that conserves resources or the animal's energy is called resource conservation.

Polar bears have adapted to conserve heat. Their guard hairs are hollow and work like insulation to store body heat.

3

AMAZING ADAPTATIONS

These animals have adapted in different ways to conserve resources.

Squirrels

Squirrels conserve resources by storing food. They bury enough nuts and seeds to help them to survive winter. Squirrels have a very good sense of smell, so they can locate their buried food even through deep snow.

Koala

Koalas eat only the leaves of the eucalyptus tree. These leaves are hard to digest and provide very little energy. To conserve energy, koalas have adapted by sleeping 18 to 22 hours a day. This saves energy for digesting their plant diet.

Black Bears

Black bears hibernate in winter. Hibernation is a long period of deep sleep that allows animals to conserve energy when food is scarce. Black bears can sleep for up to seven months without eating or drinking.

What Is Resource Conservation?

Resource conservation means making the most of the resources the animal needs to survive and using as little as possible. These resources are energy, food, and water. There are many ways of conserving resources. One of the easiest ways to conserve energy is to be inactive, for example. Storing fat in the body is one way to conserve food.

HOT CLIMATE

Deserts are very hot during the day. Most desert animals have developed ways to avoid becoming too hot. Rattlesnakes are active only at dawn and dusk, when the temperature is cooler. At night, when the desert is very cold, desert animals need to conserve heat. Animals that live in deserts also need to conserve water. They do not sweat much. Some have adapted to get enough water from their food. They do not need to drink very often.

COLD CLIMATE

Animals that live in cold areas have adapted to have thick coats in winter to protect them from the cold. This helps them to conserve heat and energy. Polar bears have a thick layer of special fat called blubber that keeps them warm. Many animals hibernate in winter when food resources are limited.

Fennec foxes live in hot desert environments in North Africa. Their big ears lose body heat more quickly than small ears. This helps keep the foxes cool. Their long, thick fur keeps them warm on cold nights and protects them from heat during the day. Like many desert animals, fennec foxes can go for long periods without water. They have several adaptations to help them conserve water. They stay cool living in underground dens. They are active at night, instead of during the heat of the day.

By working together to look after their young and protect each other, fennec foxes conserve energy.

How Do Animals Use Resource Conservation?

Animals use resource conservation to survive in environments where resources are scarce. Animals conserve energy by finding ways of staying warm or cool. **Camouflage** is another way to conserve energy. Animals that can hide from their predators do not have to expend energy on outrunning them. The white coat of the arctic hare is a form of camouflage. It blends into the white snow of the hare's habitat.

Conserving food resources may mean storing fat reserves in their bodies or storing food supplies in their habitats. Leopards and foxes sometimes catch larger prey than they can eat at one time. They bury or hide the rest and return to eat it later.

Animals have adapted in many ways to conserve water. Some animals have adapted their diet to get the water they need from their food. Others have bodies that need very little water.

Some animals have adapted to save energy when it is cold outside. Dormice sleep for most of the day over a period of several months. This is called torpor.

Conserving Resources in an Arctic Food Pyramid

Resource conservation plays an important role for all animals in a food pyramid. The snowy owl is a **tertiary consumer**. With thick feathers covering its body from head to foot, this owl is well adapted to its environment. The Arctic fox is a **secondary consumer**. Its short muzzle, small ears, and the fur on the soles of its feet are adaptations that help it keep warm in the cold Arctic climate. The Arctic squirrel is a **primary consumer**. It eats plants, which are **producers**.

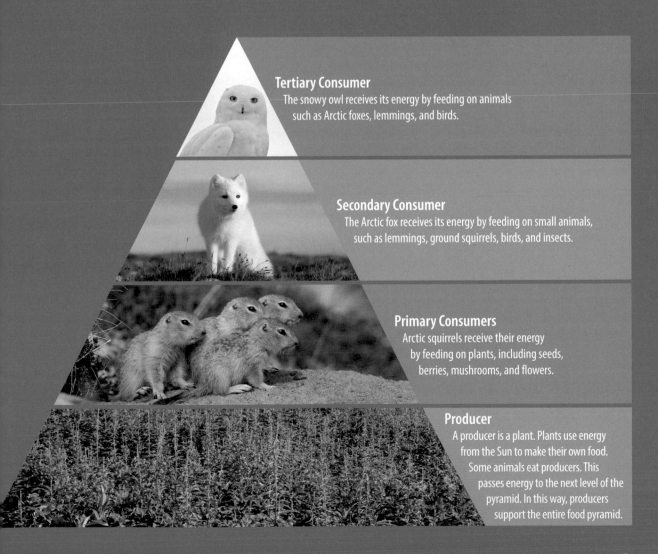

Tertiary Consumer
The snowy owl receives its energy by feeding on animals such as Arctic foxes, lemmings, and birds.

Secondary Consumer
The Arctic fox receives its energy by feeding on small animals, such as lemmings, ground squirrels, birds, and insects.

Primary Consumers
Arctic squirrels receive their energy by feeding on plants, including seeds, berries, mushrooms, and flowers.

Producer
A producer is a plant. Plants use energy from the Sun to make their own food. Some animals eat producers. This passes energy to the next level of the pyramid. In this way, producers support the entire food pyramid.

Types of Resource Conservation

There are three main types of resource conservation. The first is adaptation of body structure. Ear size is an example of this type of resource conservation adaptation. Animals that live in hot climates, such as jackrabbits, have big ears to release body heat. Animals that live in cold climates, such as Arctic fox, have small ears to conserve heat.

The second type of resource conservation is adaptation of an animal's body system. The antifreeze in the blood of Antarctic fish is an example of a body system adapting to an extremely cold habitat. It keeps the fish from freezing solid.

The third type of resource conservation is adaptation of behavior. Hummingbirds, for example, have adapted to be active only during the day. If they were active in the cold night air, their bodies would lose heat so quickly they would die. Instead, the birds go into torpor each night.

Hummingbirds use a huge amount of energy, constantly flapping their wings at high speed. These tiny birds need more than their own body weight in food each day.

3

TYPES OF RESOURCE CONSERVATION

Adaptation of Behavior

One example of behavior adaptation is being active only at night. This is a typical adaptation of desert animals to avoid hot daytime temperatures. Many species of snakes and lizards are active only in the dark.

Adaptation of Body Structure

One example of a body structure adaptation is the fur of musk oxen. Their long, shaggy coat keeps them warm. A fleecy undercoat adds insulation in the winter, but sheds in the summer.

Adaptation of Body Systems

When bar-headed geese migrate, they cross the Himalayas, which are the highest mountains in the world. At such high altitudes, there is very little oxygen in the air. The hearts and lungs of the geese are adapted to cope with low oxygen levels.

How Does It Work?

Animals may adapt to conserve body heat and stay warm by growing thick fur or thick layers of fat. Other animals migrate to warmer climates for the winter. Another way for an animal to save energy and food in winter is to hibernate. Stored body fat keeps the animal alive while it sleeps. Its body temperature falls and its heartbeat and breathing slow down, meaning less energy is used.

To stay cool in hot climates, many animals simply avoid the hot times of the day. Some are nocturnal, or only active at night. Others like the bobcat are crepuscular, or active at dawn and dusk. Some animals live in burrows underground where it is cooler.

Desert animals have different ways of coping with lack of water. Some, such as the kangaroo rat, have body systems that lose hardly any water when they get rid of waste products. Many desert animals drink very little if any water. They get most or all of the water they need from the foods they eat.

Some birds and rodents conserve resources by storing food for the winter in different places. This is called scatter hoarding. Jays and chickadees do this.

4 ADAPTATIONS THAT HELP ANIMALS CONSERVE THEIR RESOURCES

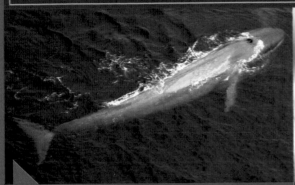

Fat Storage

The fat layer, or blubber of a blue whale, can be 14 inches (35 centimeters) thick. It keeps the whales warm in icy water. It also stores energy for the whales to use on their long migrations.

Retaining Water

The dorcas gazelle will drink if water is available. However, it can go its whole life without drinking because it gets all the liquid it needs from its food. It loses hardly any water through body waste.

Deep Hibernation

The wood frog adapts to the Arctic winter by going into deep hibernation. Nearly 70 percent of the water in its body freezes. Special substances in the frog's blood protect it from freezing solid. In spring, the frog wakes up and thaws out.

Keeping Cool

In hot climates, animals need to keep cool. An African elephant has very large ears. The large surface area of its ears helps the elephant lose body heat. This helps to lower its body temperature and keep the elephant cool.

Timeline

Earth has changed in many ways over millions of years. Some species have adapted to these changes and survived. Others have become **extinct**. The modern camel is a highly specialized animal. There are two types of camel. The dromedary camel lives in northern Africa and the Middle East and has one hump. The Bactrian camel has two humps and shaggy hair and lives in Asia. All camels have a common **ancestor**.

BACTRIAN CAMEL

A Bactrian camel's thick, shaggy coat protects it from the intense cold in winter. In summer, the hair thins out.

DROMEDARY CAMEL

A dromedary camel can live for several weeks without water. When it does fill up, it can drink 30 gallons (114 liters) in 15 minutes. A camel's hump is filled with fat, which converts to energy and water when it is needed.

Camel Adaptations

45 million years ago

The earliest known camel is the Peterson's camel. It is the size of a rabbit and lives in the forests of North America.

3.5 million years ago

The giant camel lives in North America. It is the size of a giraffe. The giant camel spreads to parts of Europe and Asia.

10,000 years ago

Camels become extinct in North America. Only two species survive, one in Asia and one in northern Africa. Camels adapt to living in deserts and on dry grasslands.

4,500 to 5,000 years ago

Camels become **domesticated**. They are used for transportation, milk, and warfare.

Today

There are about 13 million camels in the world. Most of these are domesticated and most are dromedaries. There are about 300,000 wild camels in the Australian desert.

How Humans Use Resource Conservation

People have learned from observing how animals have adapted to their environments. They have used this knowledge to develop useful technology to benefit society. Scientists and inventors have created many tools and equipment based on this technology.

Once humans started to grow their food, they began to live in settlements. They learned from animals about storing food. This was very important for winter or in times of **drought**, when crops might fail. People learned how to preserve food by keeping it in a cool place. When scientists invented refrigeration, food could be stored for longer periods. When trucks with refrigeration were developed, it became possible to transport foods over long distances.

With refrigeration, foods are now available in places where they cannot be grown.

People learned from animals about keeping warm in a cold environment. They learned to use animal fur to stay warm. People also learned from animals how to cope in the heat. In countries with hot climates, people often rest or sleep in the early afternoon. A rest like this during the hottest part of the day is called a siesta. It lets people conserve energy. Their bodies do not have to work so hard to stay cool.

People who live in cold regions, such as the Arctic, may wear animal fur to help them conserve heat.

Some people in hot regions live in caves. This keeps them cool and conserves energy.

Resource Conservation and Biodiversity

Biodiversity refers to the variety of life in a habitat or **biome**. Biomes include aquatic, desert, forest, and grassland habitats. Many animals develop unique adaptations for the habitat they live in. The survival of many species depends on biodiversity. A greater variety of animals and plants in an area creates a stronger food chain.

Penguins keep their body temperatures high so they can stay active in their ice cold habitat. Their feathers are very tightly packed and made waterproof by oil from their bodies. They have blubber under their thick skin. The dark feathers on a penguin's back absorb heat from the Sun.

Penguins huddle together in large groups to conserve heat.

Gila monsters are large lizards living in the deserts of Mexico and the southeastern United States. They spend much of their lives in underground burrows to avoid the desert heat. They can store fat in their tails. They are able to live for months without eating.

Gila monsters may eat only three or four times a year. They can eat up to one-third of their body weight in one meal.

Conservation

Animal adaptations take thousands of years to develop. Many animals are specially adapted to living in a certain environment. They may not be able to survive anywhere else. If their environment changes, the animals could become extinct.

Earth's climate is getting warmer. This is causing the ice in the **polar regions** to melt at a fast rate. That could affect the animals that live there. Human populations in desert areas are growing and using up water resources needed by the animals. There are many organizations working to protect the environment against these threats by human activity. The World Wildlife Fund and the International Union for Conservation of Nature are two such groups. They are working with governments and industry to find solutions for this problem.

Scientists study the ice in polar regions to see how fast it is melting. If too much ice melts, the animals that live in these places may not be able to survive.

Activity

Match each animal with the type of resource conservation that helps it to survive.

1 Blue whale

2 Black bear

3 Dorcas gazelle

4 Squirrel

A Hibernation

B Water from food

C Storing food for winter

D Blubber

Answers: 1. D 2. A 3. B 4. C

Quiz

Complete this quiz to test your knowledge of resource conservation.

1 What is biodiversity?

A. The variety of life in a habitat or biome

2 How do an elephant's large ears help to keep it cool?

A. The large surface area of their ears helps them to lose body heat

3 How does the koala conserve energy?

A. By sleeping 18 to 22 hours a day

4 Where do Gila monsters store fat?

A. In their tails

5 What does it mean if an animal is nocturnal?

A. It is active only at night

6 Where does the fennec fox live?

A. North Africa

7 Where do some people in hot places live to stay cool?

A. In caves

8 What type of camel has two humps?

A. The Bactrian camel

9 How does blubber help polar bears and penguins conserve energy?

A. It keeps them warm in their icy habitat

10 What is torpor?

A. When animals sleep most of the day over a period of several months

Key Words

ancestor: animals of the same species that have come before

biome: a large community of plants and animals that live in a major habitat, such as a forest

camouflage: color or patterns on an animal's fur, skin, or feathers that help it blend in with its surroundings

deserts: dry areas with very little rainfall or vegetation

domesticated: trained to live and work with people

drought: a long period without rain

extinct: when all members of a species have died out

genes: the parts of a cell that control appearance and inherited behavior in living things

habitat: the natural environment of a living thing

natural selection: a process whereby animals that have better adapted to their environment survive and pass on those adaptations to their young

polar regions: the areas surrounding the North Pole and the South Pole

primary consumer: an animal that eats producers, or plants

producers: plants which receive their energy from the Sun and provide food for animals

secondary consumer: an animal that feeds on plant-eating animals

species: a group of plants or animals that are alike

tertiary consumer: a meat eater at the top of the food chain

Index

Africa 7, 13, 14, 15, 22
Arctic 8, 9, 10, 13, 17
Asia 14, 15
Australia 15

bears 4, 5, 6, 21, 22
berries 9
biodiversity 18, 22
biomes 18, 22
birds 9, 10, 12
blubber 6, 13, 18, 21, 22

camels 14, 15, 22

deserts 6, 7, 11, 12, 15, 18, 19, 20
dormice 8, 22

elephants 13, 22

flowers 9
food pyramid 9
forests 15, 18
foxes 7, 8, 9, 10, 22

frogs 13

gazelles 13, 21
Gila monsters 19, 22
grasslands 15, 18

habitats 4, 8, 10, 18, 22
hibernation 5, 6, 12, 13, 21

ice 20
insects 9
International Union for Conservation of Nature 20

kangaroo rats 12
koalas 5, 22

lemmings 9
leopards 8
lizards 11, 19

Mexico 19
Middle East 14

mushrooms 9
musk oxen 11

North America 15

owls 9

penguins 18, 22
plants 5, 9, 18

refrigeration 16

seeds 5, 9
snakes 6, 11
squirrels 5, 9, 21
Sun 9, 18

United States 19

whales 13, 21
World Wildlife Fund 20

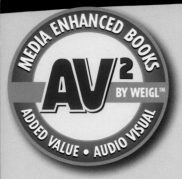

Log on to www.av2books.com

AV² by Weigl brings you media enhanced books that support active learning. Go to www.av2books.com, and enter the special code found on page 2 of this book. You will gain access to enriched and enhanced content that supplements and complements this book. Content includes video, audio, weblinks, quizzes, a slide show, and activities.

AV² Online Navigation

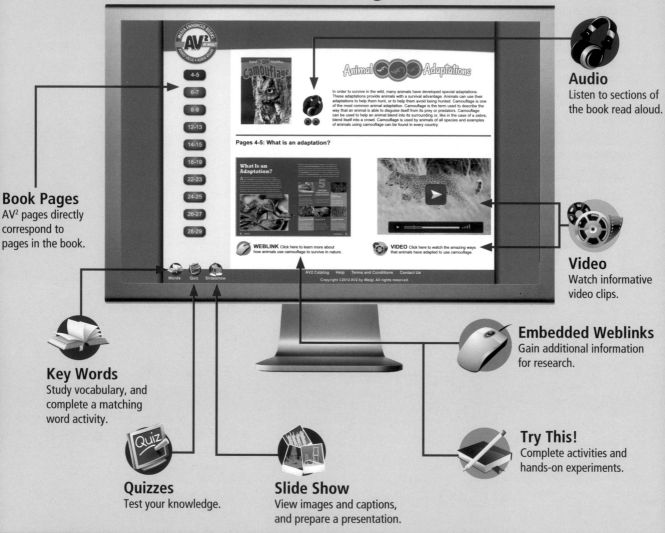

Book Pages
AV² pages directly correspond to pages in the book.

Audio
Listen to sections of the book read aloud.

Video
Watch informative video clips.

Key Words
Study vocabulary, and complete a matching word activity.

Embedded Weblinks
Gain additional information for research.

Quizzes
Test your knowledge.

Slide Show
View images and captions, and prepare a presentation.

Try This!
Complete activities and hands-on experiments.

AV² was built to bridge the gap between print and digital. We encourage you to tell us what you like and what you want to see in the future.

Sign up to be an AV² Ambassador at www.av2books.com/ambassador.

Due to the dynamic nature of the internet, some of the URLs and activities provided as part of AV² by Weigl may have changed or ceased to exist. AV² by Weigl accepts no responsibility for any such changes. All media enhanced books are regularly monitored to update addresses and sites in a timely manner. Contact AV² by Weigl at 1-866-649-3445 or av2books@weigl.com with any questions, comments, or feedback.